331.01

WITHDRAWN 15/3/

D0476746

THOMAS TALLIS SCHOOL LIBRARY

018219

What do we mean by
human rights?

Workers'
Rights

Katherine Prior

FRANKLIN WATTS
LONDON • SYDNEY

Revised and updated 2004

Franklin Watts
96 Leonard Street,
London
EC2A 4XD

Franklin Watts Australia
44-51 Huntley Street,
Alexandria
NSW 2015

© Franklin Watts 1997, 2004

Series editor: Rachel Cooke
Art Director: Robert Walster
Designer: Simon Borrough
Picture research: Sarah Moule
Consultants: Cristina Sganga and
Dan Jones of Amnesty International

A CIP catalogue record for this book
is available from the British Library.

ISBN 0 7496 5904 1

Dewey Classification 331.88

Printed in Malaysia

Acknowledgements:
Case studies: Tower Colliery, The
Independent, 12 January 1996, S2 pp. 2-
3; The Guardian, 29 April 1995, p. 25;
http://www.christian-
air.org.uk/afghanistan/harvest/0208area.
htm; http://www.heritagekonpa.
com/archieves/Haiti%20slave%20child%
20labor.htm; Taiwanese women workers,
The Guardian, 12 October 1994, p. 12
G2T; Sydney, women's pay, Jill Ker
Conway, The Road from Coorain
(London, 1989); German construction
workers, The Guardian, 2 October 1995,
p. 6; http://www.tuc. org.uk/
international/tuc-6850-f0.cfm Indonesia,
The Economist, 9 July 1994, p. 66; New
Internationalist, January 1995, p. 12;
Brazil Information from Oxfam: Brazil
(Oxford: 1995); http://workhealth.org/
whatsnew/lpkarosh.html; The Guardian,
30 March 1996, p. 1.

Picture credits:

The authors would like to thank the
following for their permission to
reproduce the photographs in this
book:

Cover and contents page:
Network/Laurie Sparham
Insides:
Andes Press Agency/Carlos Reyes-
Manzo 30
Mary Evans Picture Library 15B, 35T,
38B
Robert Harding Picture Library 43T;
D. Beatty 43B; Bildagentur Schuster/
Bramaz 6B; M. Jenner 37T; P. Van Riel
21T; West Light/P. Kopp 28B
Hutchison Library 10, 18; R.
Aberman 28T; D. Cliverd 11T; R.
Francis 6T; S. McBride 24T; Pern 7B
The Image Bank/F. Chalfant 7T;
J.P. Kelly 27T; S. Niedorf 8B;
A. Pistolesi 37BR
Image Select/Ann Ronan 17B
Magnum Pictures/I. Berry 40L;
R. Rai 19B, 42
Mansell Collection 31B
Network/J. Matthews 14R
Panos Pictures/T. Bolstad 17T, 39,
41B; D. Constantine 23T; N. Cooper
12B, 27B, 32B ; R. Giling 34T;
G. Mansfield 11B; N. Peachey 13T;
D. Reed 40R; N. Robinson 20T;
P. Smith 36T; S. Sprague 12T, 13B;
B. Stephenson 20/21; C. Stowers 22;
P. Tweedie 9B, 29;
Popperfoto 26T; AFP/Khan 15T
Rex Features Ltd. 31T, 34B;
N. Berman 35B; P. Brown 41T;
Ende-ZNZ 36B; L. Oy 23B; SIPA 37BL
Frank Spooner/Gamma-Liaison/
Halebian 24/5; F. Savariau 33
Topham Picturepoint/AP 9T
Trip/M. Lee 20C; H. Rogers 32T;
J. Wakelin 8T, 16
ZEFA 26B; G. Heil 14L; Norman 38T

CONTENTS

As a small child were you ever asked 'What do you want to be when you grow up?'. It seems such a simple question, and the people who ask it always expect you to say something straightforward like 'a firefighter' or 'a nurse'. But work is not simple. Imagine if you had said that you wanted to be a cook. This might mean anything from someone who makes burgers in a fast-food shop to a top chef who commands a vast workforce of undercooks in a gleaming restaurant kitchen. Both workers are cooks, but the first one has few skills and is poorly paid, while the second one has years of training and experience and is rewarded handsomely by the restaurant owners.

A question of skills

This book looks at the ways workers are treated in different industries and professions around the world. The difference between low-skilled and skilled workers, like the two cooks, is fundamental to

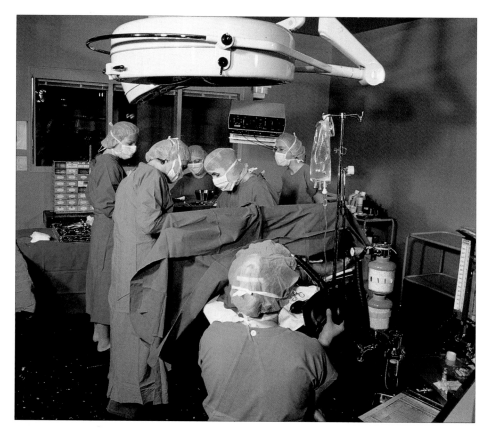

workers' experiences. A skill is a technique or knowledge that a person acquires enabling them to do particular tasks. It can be a simple skill, like knowing how to fry a burger, or a complex system of interlocking knowledge and techniques, like knowing how to do brain surgery. The more skilled a worker is, the more he or she may be paid by an employer.

Workers are also differentiated by the type of work they do. Jobs which require more physical strength than creative thought or initiative are called manual jobs or blue-collar jobs – after the blue, protective overalls that

Blue-collar workers like builders' labourers (top) require strength and physical endurance for their work. Skilled professionals, such as surgeons and anaesthetists (bottom), require years of training and study for their work.

Architects are white-collar workers. They design buildings and, unlike the workers who build them, usually work in a clean office environment.

factory workers often wear. In contrast, white-collar jobs are those where a worker is employed in an office and, instead of physical labour, uses intellectual skills, such as maths and the ability to compose letters. These skills usually result in white-collar workers being better paid than blue-collar workers.

Industrialized nations

Most of the industrialized nations of the world are wealthy and the majority of their citizens enjoy a comfortable standard of living. They include the countries of Western Europe, Canada and the United States of America, Japan, Australia and New Zealand. Much of Eastern Europe and the former Soviet Union is industrialized as well, but these countries are much less wealthy. In an industrialized country most of the population is employed in towns and cities in manufacturing jobs or service industries, like banking, law, commerce and tourism. The agriculture in industrialized countries is highly mechanized and employs a relatively small number of people.

Developing nations

In countries that are not industrialized the pattern of employment is reversed. Until recently, most of the people were engaged in labour-intensive agriculture. Now growing unemployment has caused many to move to the cities in search of work. Industry is expanding but factories and service industries employ only a small percentage of the population. These nations are often called developing nations or the 'Third World'. They include most of the countries of Africa, Latin America and Asia. Some have the potential for great wealth and some of their individual citizens are extremely rich indeed. On average, however, the people are poor and have a low standard of living.

In industrial countries agriculture is mechanized. In poorer countries, however, much of the farming work is still done by hand. These workers are rice farmers from India.

Newly industrializing countries

In the last thirty years some countries in Asia have undergone speedy industrialization. They are referred to as newly industrializing countries (NICs). They include South Korea, Taiwan, Thailand and Indonesia. Society in these countries is changing rapidly. Workers are being squeezed out of the countryside and into the multiplying factories of the cities. Although these countries are getting richer, the new wealth has not yet reached many individual workers.

Workers in newly industrializing countries are often poorly paid, making low-priced goods for export. This Chinese woman works long hours at hand-embroidery to make enough to live on and may suffer eye damage and back strain as a result.

'everyone has the right to work'

In the last thirty years, South Korea's economy has grown rapidly, fuelled by the hard work of its blue-collar workers in electronics production like this computer factory.

A set of rules for everyone

When we look at the differences between workers in the world it often seems that there is one rule for the rich and another for the poor. The Universal Declaration of Human Rights was adopted by the United Nations in 1948. Its purpose was to create one set of standards for all people in the world, whether rich or poor. Work takes up most of our lives and many of the rights spelt out in the Declaration specifically concern workers and the workplace (see panel). This book examines how much progress the world has made in achieving those rights and considers what remains to be done.

The United Nations brings together representatives of independent nations from all over the world. In 1948, after the horrors of the Second World War, it adopted a declaration of human rights designed to protect people throughout the world.

Workers' rights

These are some of the key clauses of the Universal Declaration of Human Rights that are concerned with work.

Article 4
No one shall be held in slavery or servitude; slavery and the slave trade shall be prohibited in all their forms.

Article 23
(1) Everyone has the right to work, to free choice of employment, to just and favourable conditions of work and to protection against unemployment.
(2) Everyone, without any discrimination, has the right to equal pay for equal work.
(3) Everyone who works has the right to just and favourable remuneration ensuring for himself and his family an existence worthy of human dignity, and supplemented, if necessary, by other means of social protection.
(4) Everyone has the right to form and to join trade unions for the protection of his interests.

Article 24
Everyone has the right to rest and leisure, including reasonable limitation of working hours and periodic holidays with pay.

Many workers, like these men in a plastics factory, use dangerous machinery every day. Article 23 of the Universal Declaration of Human Rights guarantees the right to favourable working conditions, which includes providing a safe working environment.

Date:
1 January 1995
Place:
Tower Colliery,
Rhonda Valley,
South Wales, UK
Issue:
A local fight
against
unemployment

Tower Colliery is a shallow coal mine in south Wales in Britain. For over 150 years local boys expected to get a job at the mine after leaving school, but in 1993 the mine's owners announced that they were closing it. Each miner was offered £20,000 or more in compensation, but there were to be no more jobs.

Tower Colliery was the biggest employer in the area and its closure threatened the whole community's way of life. Local shops could only survive if people had money to buy things from them. Without any chance of a job, young people would leave the area and facilities like schools, banks and post-offices would close because not enough people were using them. Every closure would mean the loss of more jobs.

Faced with such a grim future, the miners decided to use their redundancy money to buy the

In much of Europe and North America the old jobs in mining and heavy industry are dying out, threatening whole communities.

mine and run it for themselves. It now has a regular turnover of £25 million, with some 300 employees who are all shareholders. By keeping the mine open and making it more profitable, they have saved jobs for the whole community.

'the biggest employer in the area'

Disappearing jobs

Over the last 20 years thousands of people in industrialized countries have lost their jobs to new technology – from cash-dispensing machines to automated garbage trucks. In addition, factory jobs have dwindled as manufacturers have moved their production to Asia and North Africa where labour is cheap.

a 'job for everyone'

018219

Machines now do many of the jobs that people once did. This modern rubbish collection van needs just one or two men to operate it, instead of a whole team.

The right to work

Work gives people independence: earning a wage means that you do not have to rely on your family or the government for food and housing. This is why the right to work is recognized as a basic human right. To meet this right governments have to ensure that there are enough jobs in their country for their citizens. They have a duty to keep unemployment as low as possible. This does not just mean physically providing jobs but by creating the right circumstances where individual initiatives, such as Tower Colliery, can prosper.

Most of these disappearing jobs are blue-collar jobs which require few skills. Many of the people who did them have been unable to get jobs in new industries like information technology, telecommunications and tourism, which require a higher level of education and a wider range of skills. Governments in industrialized countries are therefore encouraging their young people to stay longer in education and to learn things like word-processing, marketing and computer-aided design. But unemployment continues to be a problem – many of the political debates today centre around the best way to create a 'job for everyone'.

Children in the developed world are now being taught skills such as using computers from an early age. This is to prepare them for the type of work which will be available to them later in life.

Date:
2002
Place:
Agricultural Cooperative, Afghanistan
Issue:
Working together

Mirza Abdul Haq suffered with his fellow farmers in western Afghanistan during years of severe drought. It reduced the land they could cultivate down to 4%. The wheat would grow two feet, but the river would run dry and the crop could not be harvested. They had only a bull to work the land.

Then help came from the Agency for Rehabilitation and Energy conservation in Afghanistan (AREA), an agricultural cooperative. It contributed two wells and the villagers paid for two more. AREA helped buy a tractor and activate a generator, providing electricity for the first time. By 2002, the crops were growing on 30% of the land.

Mirza, now treasurer of the cooperative, harvested wheat for the first time in four years. He said the villagers would have fled to a displaced persons' camp or even Iran if AREA was not there. 'We are grateful for your help,' he told them, 'because otherwise we couldn't survive.'

(Top and right). By combining modern tools with traditional skills in co-operatives, many people all over the world can work to earn a secure income.

This young Bangladeshi man makes a living from collecting and selling used oil barrels. It is hard work and, if he falls sick or has an accident with his cart, he loses his income.

No skills, no security

Unemployment in poor countries is harder to measure than in rich countries – it is not always obvious whether someone has a regular job or not. Many poor people in Asia, Africa, Latin America and Eastern Europe work hard, but they lack the security of permanent employment and fair wages which would allow them a good standard of living. In that sense, their right to work has not been fulfilled. Often leaving school at an early age and with few skills, they end up in badly paid casual jobs, which means they are always vulnerable: an accident or illness can reduce them to destitution.

Co-operatives, such as the one in Shoa, are one way forward in creating and sustaining employment but can only be part of the solution. As in the developed world, the burden of upholding the right to work falls on the government, but few developing countries have the financial resources necessary. These governments can afford little long-term investment in schemes to create work and most are unable to pay welfare or social security benefits to all their citizens when they are out of work or unable to make enough money to ensure 'an existence worthy of human dignity'.

'an existence worthy of human dignity'

In a poor country which cannot afford to provide social security benefits, people without professional skills can easily be reduced to begging, like this mother and child in Brazil.

Place:
Acailandia, Brazil
Issue:
The free choice of employment

The city of Acailandia is surrounded by iron-smelting factories and charcoal estates. Charcoal is the fuel used to smelt iron. Making it is hard, dirty work. It is produced by slowly burning wood in mud kilns. The workers suffer burns, cuts and splinters and the ash clogs up their lungs. Their clothes and skin are black with grime. Few people like the work and the pay is poor, so why do they do it?

Many of the workers are from elsewhere in Brazil. They have been tricked into the job by labour contractors promising them high wages as charcoal-burners. On arrival, however, the new workers often discover that the pay is lower than promised and that the contractor has charged them for transporting them to the estate. They must pay off this debt before they can leave.

'They are trapped'

On some estates the workers are paid in vouchers, not cash, which can only be exchanged for overpriced goods at a store owned by the estate. The workers spend all of their earnings just on food. They are trapped. Most cannot leave because they cannot save enough money to pay off the contractor. Those who try to escape risk being beaten up or even killed.

Brazilian charcoal estates have been described as 'hell on earth'. Whole families live and work amongst the hot, smouldering charcoal kilns, breathing in noxious fumes and ash.

This man works at the charcoal kilns that produce fuel for iron-ore smelting in Acailandia, Brazil.

This woman brick-maker works in Islamabad, Pakistan. A bonded labourer, she is not free to change her job. Without education, her little boy will probably suffer the same fate.

Debt bondage: a form of slavery

How would you feel if a neighbour offered you £5.00 to mow his lawn but, when you had finished, said he would pay you only £2.00? Worse still, what if he then said that he was charging you £3.00 for hiring his lawn-mower, so that you actually owed him £1.00 and would now have to wash his car to pay off the debt? After mowing a lawn and washing a car, you would still not have received any money.

This may seem incredible, but it is exactly the sort of trick that has been played on the Brazilian charcoal-workers. Where workers are made to go on working for an employer to pay off a never-ending debt, this is called debt bondage. They are like slaves because their freedom to decide how and where they work has been destroyed.

The survival of slavery

Most people assume that slavery ended in the 19th century, but even today there are many jobs where workers have so little freedom that they are no better than slaves. Several million workers around the world are held in conditions of slavery or near slavery. These include domestic servants in Colombia, agricultural labourers in Pakistan, gemstone polishers in India and salt miners in the Sahara desert.

Slaves on a plantation in 19th-century Brazil are punished by their white owner for minor offences. Images like this convey the horror of slavery but few people realize it continues today.

Date:
2003
Place:
Port-au-Prince,
Haiti
Issue:
Domestic
servitude

Madeleine Vilma, 15, lives on the streets of the Haitian capital because she was tortured and beaten by her domestic employers. She had been forced into work at the age of 9, when her parents could not even feed her. A middleman traded her into a household for a small sum, and Madeleine had to work hard as a maid for her food and shelter, but no pay. She told the Los Angeles Times of a punishment she had received for just breaking a heel off her shoe. The two women employers, Auntie and Maman, beat her with their sandals and then gave jolts to her chest and arms with a frayed electrical cord. 'They wanted to mark me so that I would remember,' she said.

Madeleine is only one of Haiti's estimated 300,000 domestic slave children who are called restaveks, a name derived from the French words rester avec, meaning 'to stay with'. Rural children as young as 4 are taken into the cities to begin work. Their employers are almost always low-income families. Foreign relief workers and charities are seeking out the restaveks to offer them shelter, hot meals and schooling. These relief workers have faced violence when going to various homes. In 2003, the Haitian Parliament finally passed a law that restricts the use of these domestic slave servants.

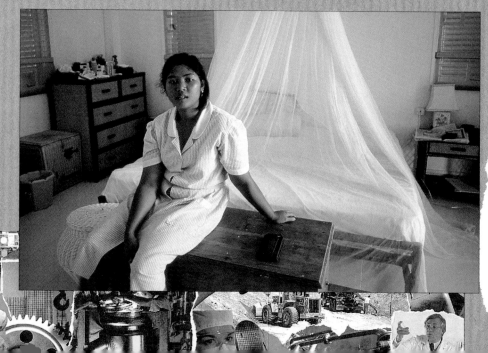

The right to accept and reject a job

Slavery has been outlawed by nearly every country in the world. The Universal Declaration of Human Rights states that no one shall be held in slavery. It also says everyone has the right to free choice of employment. This means that someone must not be tricked into a job by false promises or forced to work by the threat of violence or perpetual debt.

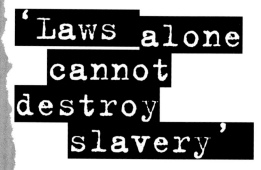

'Laws alone cannot destroy slavery'

Workers who wish to leave their jobs may have to give several weeks' notice or warning to their employer. Essentially, however, the right to a free choice of job means also the right to leave it. The freedom of workers to reject unattractive jobs is an incentive for employers to look after their workers.

Breaking out of domestic servitude can be very difficult. Many women are forced to live in poor conditions and to work for little or no pay.

Can slavery be stopped?

Most slavery survives in poor countries where widespread poverty means that there are people who are easily trapped by debt. It flourishes in remote rural areas where workers are beyond the reach of trade unions and in areas where government control is weak and wealthy employers and landowners can bribe the police to ignore how they treat their workers. Laws alone cannot destroy slavery. Governments have to act on them, tracking down and prosecuting guilty employers, no matter how rich or powerful they are.

Poor, unskilled people are most likely to become trapped by debt and often they do not know their legal rights. This quarry-worker in India has been a bonded labourer for 30 years.

Slavery today may not be as obvious as in the past, when the trade was widespread, but it is equally cruel and inhumane.

Date:
19 November 1993
Place:
Zhili Toy Factory, Shenzhen, China
Issue:
Workers' safety

Toy factories, like this doll workshop in China, pose big fire hazards because of the inflammable fabrics, plastics, paints and stuffing stockpiled in them.

The Zhili toy factory in China used to employ several hundred workers, mostly young women. The factory was like a jail. The manager kept the doors locked so that the women could not take a break without him noticing and even the windows were barred with heavy metal grilles.

On 19 November 1993 a fire broke out and quickly spread through the factory. The workers were trapped as thick black smoke billowed up the stairways. Desperately, they tried to find unlocked doors. Some were trampled to death in the rush to get out. Others choked on the poisonous fumes. In total, 81 workers were killed.

'owners ignored the warning'

These workers died because their employers did not observe safety precautions. Only a few months before the fire, the Shenzhen fire department had inspected the factory and advised its owners to make safety improvements, but the owners had ignored the warning. The fire started because the factory's electrical circuits were faulty. Once ablaze it spread rapidly because there were no fire-proof doors to hold back the fire. There were too few exits and many of these were locked, trapping people inside. The workers had no fire-safety training; instead of evacuating the building calmly, they trampled one another in the hurry to get out.

The price of safety

Look at the label of any soft toy and see if it says anything about safety. Toys sold in the developed world must meet certain safety standards so that parents can be sure that their children will not be hurt by them. Unfortunately, the workers who make the toys are often not as well protected: most soft toys are made in Asia, where international toy companies build their factories because production costs are low – partly because the laws on factory safety are poorly enforced.

In 1993 almost 2,500 workers were killed in factory fires in China. In Thailand, in May 1993 a dreadful fire at the Kader toy factory killed 189 workers. Like the Chinese fires, it happened because the factory's owners refused to spend enough money on safety.

A safe working environment

The Universal Declaration of Human Rights states that every worker has the right to 'favourable conditions of work'. This means, first of all, a workplace that is safe. It means that workers should be able to trust that the machinery and materials they work with are safe and that their building is not a fire-trap. It means, too, that employers must take all possible measures to protect their workers from danger. An employer must not put the health of a worker at risk in order to save money.

A teddy is the image of safety and comfort, but not always for the workers who make them in the factories of China and South-East Asia.

One of the world's worst industrial disasters was a poisonous gas-leak from the Union Carbide factory in Bhopal in India in 1984. Thousands of people died and many more suffered horrendous injuries, including being blinded, like these people here. Today the people of Bhopal are still fighting in the courts for compensation for their suffering and for adequate health care to cope with the appalling legacy of the accident.

How to enforce safety laws?

Most governments have laws to protect workers' safety and to prosecute employers who endanger the lives of their workers. In a poor country, however, like China or Thailand, these laws are rarely enforced because the government worries that the resulting increase in production costs will cause factory-owners to move on to other countries. Both China and Thailand have millions of people who need jobs in the toy factories; they cannot afford to see these jobs go elsewhere.

Therefore it is up to the countries who buy the toys to say that they will only buy from companies that treat their workers properly. After the 1993 fires some toy importers in Europe agreed to stop importing 'dirty toys'.

Safety standards often differ for workers in rich and poor countries. The welder in Uganda (above) only has sunglasses to protect his eyes. He has no protective clothing, gloves or shoes. The welder in Britain (right) is well protected.

Workers' responsibility

Workers have a role to play in ensuring their own safety at work. For example, on building sites employers should issue their workers with protective clothing, such as hard-hats. Workers have an obligation to use these items which have been provided for their protection.

Employers have to ensure that their workers use these items: if they don't, the employers become responsible for breaking safety regulations and may be sued for an injury caused to a worker.

Date:
2001
Place:
American Samoa
Issue:
Working and living conditions

The Daewoosa factory in American Samoa, a Pacific territory of the USA, made clothes for several US companies, such as Target and J C Penney. Its Vietnamese workers, who were 90 per cent women, were forced to live in cramped living quarters. They were fed rice and cabbage broth and sometimes, as punishment, received nothing to eat. One woman, waiting for fabric to arrive, was attacked by her employers and lost an eye, because they thought she was avoiding work. The employees finally won a lawsuit against the plant for nonpayment of $600,000 wages and for contract violations, but the owner did not pay and the factory went bankrupt. It was closed in January 2001 for human rights violations.

In garment factories, women machinists are often treated like parts of the sewing machines they operate, not people.

Dignity in the workplace

The right to an acceptable workplace is not just about safety. It is also about providing workers with a reasonable level of comfort and dignity. The Northsails limit on workers' trips to the toilet is cruel and undignified. It infringes their privacy and treats them as if they were machines or robots, rather than human beings. It is far from the only example of employers failing to respect their workers' dignity. In both the developed and the developing world, people often disagree what exactly a 'reasonable' level of comfort involves.

'a reasonable level of comfort'

Construction workers need to be particularly aware of their own responsibility for their safety as building sites are full of potential dangers.

21

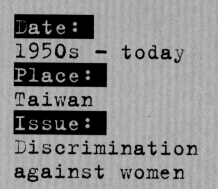

Date:
1950s – today
Place:
Taiwan
Issue:
Discrimination against women

Taiwan owes much to the hard work of its women. It is women who make the clothes, electronic items and household goods which carry the 'Made in Taiwan' label all over the world. In spite of their labour, however, the women are stuck in low-paid, unskilled jobs in factories. Most of the better paid, more highly skilled jobs in banking, computing, law and medicine go to men. The few women who do get skilled jobs are usually paid less than their male colleagues and are made to sign contracts promising that they will leave their job if they get married.

The Taiwanese Government has passed laws to protect the rights of women workers, but employers often ignore them. The law states that a woman who is having a baby should be given eight weeks off from work, with full pay, and should be able to return to her old job after her leave. Often, however, a pregnant woman is simply sacked.

It is largely due to the hard work of Taiwanese women in factories that Taiwan's economy has been so successful but they are not well rewarded for their labour.

Taiwanese women are beginning to protest about the way employers treat them. They point to the huge contribution that their labour has made to the Taiwanese economy and argue that, in return, they deserve better access to skilled jobs.

Taiwan has thrived on manufacturing. This is the largest bicycle factory in the world outside of China.

In Cambodia, land-mine victims can, with special equipment and training, become productive, self-supporting workers.

This Swedish daycare centre looks after babies while their mothers are at work, enabling women to continue their careers.

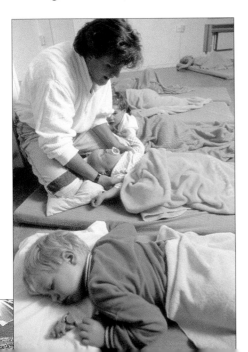

Discrimination

Most of us have been left out of something we want to be a part of, such as a sports team. But some people experience this their whole lives – simply because of their physical appearance, race or sex they can never get the job they want.

'The right to free choice of employment' does not just refer to debt bondage (see page 15). It also means that it is not fair to exclude specific groups of people from particular jobs. To respect this right, many countries have brought in anti-discrimination legislation on behalf of women, ethnic and religious minorities and people with disabilities. The legislation attempts to create an atmosphere of equal opportunities where everybody has an equal chance of getting the job they want.

Legislating for change

Effective anti-discrimination laws compel employers to change the way they employ people. For example, providing maternity leave is an essential part of preventing discrimination against women. Maternity leave allows a woman to return to her old job after she has had a baby. Without it a woman would have to start again in a new job, at the bottom of the career ladder, after each baby. She would never be able to get to the same level as her male colleagues.

Likewise, providing adequate facilities in the workplace for people with disabilities is an essential part of preventing discrimination against them. The toughest legislation requires employers to adapt their buildings for people with disabilities. This may include putting in lifts, ramps, special toilets and video telephones.

Quotas

Even with the toughest anti-discrimination legislation, many countries have found that disadvantaged workers still do not win their fair share of jobs. To combat this, some governments set targets or quotas. In Germany, for example, the government has ruled that people with disabilities should make up 6 per cent of employees in any business. It has also provided funds for training these employees.

Date:
1980s – today
Place:
Gold Mines, Witwatersrand, South Africa
Issue:
Racial discrimination against black miners

The South African economy thrives on gold mining, but until recently black miners were discriminated against. In 1987 a black miner earned, on average, only one-fifth of the wage of a white miner and the better paid, supervisory jobs were reserved exclusively for whites.

In August 1987, the South African Government abolished the law which prohibited black miners from promotion to supervisory positions and black workers can now apply for any job. But because for decades they have been denied the training and professional experience that the whites have had, blacks are finding it hard to catch up. In the gold mines black workers still earn less, on average, than white workers.

A mixed population needs a mixed workforce but what is the best way to achieve this? Here, in New York, a black policeman and a white policeman chat with a young Jewish boy.

'quotas are often controversial'

Often quotas act as guidelines only – something for an employer to aim for. But some governments make the quotas compulsory. A compulsory quota of 25 per cent of black workers, for example, would mean that a company would have to hire only black workers until they made up 25 per cent of its workforce. Compulsory quotas are often controversial. Employers feel that they are not being allowed to choose the best person for the job and other workers may complain that the disadvantaged group is getting special treatment. The quota system in some US states, where African-Americans must fill a certain percentage of public sector jobs, is attracting fierce debate, and California and Washington state have abolished it.

Advertising without discrimination

If you look at employment advertisements from the newspapers of different countries you will be able to tell how much importance each country gives to the issue of equal opportunities. In Malaysia, for example, it is still permissible to advertise for a secretary specifying that an applicant must be 'a woman, Chinese and aged under 25'. In most countries in Europe and North America specifying the sex and race of applicants would be illegal. Additionally, Australia and the USA have strict laws against age-discrimination that make it illegal to specify an applicant's preferred age.

Date:
1952
Place:
Sydney,
Australia
Issue:
Equal pay for
equal work

In 1952 an Australian school-leaver went looking for a job. Every day she read the 'Help Wanted' and 'Positions Vacant' advertisements in the Sydney newspapers. These were divided into two columns, one for men and one for women. The wages offered to women were always lower than those offered to men, even when the same job was being advertised in both columns. At the time, the girl, Jill Ker, didn't think anything of it. Like millions of other women in the world, she had grown up expecting that women earned less than men. The difference in pay, she said, 'was part of life, like the weather'.

In the 1950s, most jobs for women were in the typing pool or on a telephone switchboard. Those women searching for better paid jobs found men were chosen in preference to them.

Today, a university education can open the door to many careers, but some women with excellent qualifications still find that employers will favour men both in selecting employees and in salary levels.

'top of her year'

Eventually Jill went to university and in 1958 she graduated at the top of her year. With two boys from her class she applied to join the foreign service of the Australian Government but, although her friends got in, she was rejected because she was a woman. Suddenly she understood what the separate job advertisements had been telling her. It didn't matter how hard she worked, or how clever she was, as a woman she could not have the same career opportunities as a man.

Even in 1948, however, the picture of a male breadwinner supporting his wife was inaccurate. In Africa, Asia and Latin America, many women not only did all the housework, but also worked outside as farm-labourers, market-stall holders, building-site workers and washerwomen. Frequently women were the main or sole breadwinner in a family. It was unfair not only to them but also to their families that they should earn less than men for their hard work.

It is common in most developed countries today for both parents in a family to work.

In poor and newly industrialized countries, women do more than their fair share of housework and labouring. This young Indian woman will have to look after her family as well as doing her brick-making job.

Supporting the family

Would you think it was unfair if you did the same work as someone else, but got paid less for it? In 1948 when the United Nations declared that everyone has 'the right to equal pay for equal work', it was a radical change for most countries. Many people believed that a man should earn more than a woman because he had to support a wife and children. Women were routinely paid less than men and were expected to stop work when they got married.

27

Equal pay for work of equal value

Since 1948 many countries have passed equal pay legislation, but this has not solved all the problems of women's pay. If a man and a woman are doing the same job it is easy to compare their wages. But women and men generally have different jobs. In industrialized countries, women are usually employed in 'helping' jobs like nursing, cleaning, catering and secretarial work. In the newly industrializing countries, women are concentrated in factories. Such 'women's jobs' are poorly paid, but if no men are doing them, how can it be proved that the workers receive low wages just because they are women?

To get around this problem, some countries recognize the right of equal pay for equal value. Imagine a bakery which employs four women to do its accounts. They are paid less than the men who maintain the bakery's electricity supply. Under a law of equal pay for equal work the women could not compare their job with that of the electricians. But under a law of equal pay for equal value, they may have a chance. If they can convince an industrial tribunal that their work requires the same skill and effort as the electricians' work, then their employers will have to pay them the same rate as the electricians.

When only women do a job, as in this South African peach canning factory, it is hard to prove that they are less well paid than men doing a similar job.

'women's jobs'

Many 'caring' jobs are considered to be women's work. Nurses are often called the angels of medicine, but despite a positive image, they have had to put up with low pay and poor promotion chances.

Date:
1990s
Place:
Construction sites in Germany
Issue:
Lower pay for foreign workers

In Germany, many construction companies hire foreign workers – from places such as Poland, Portugal and Britain – because they are cheaper than local workers and accept wages below what a German worker needs to live on. In addition, the employers do not have to pay the same taxes and pension contributions on foreign workers as on German ones.

In 1995 the German government ruled that foreign workers must be paid the same rates as German workers; with high unemployment, it hoped that this would persuade construction companies to employ more Germans. Germany's building trade union said that it would not object to the foreigners if they did not undercut local wages: 'We want equal conditions for all workers; the same salary, same taxes and same social security fees.'

Immigrants, refugees and guestworkers

Women are not the only workers who suffer unequal pay. All over the world immigrants, refugees and foreign guestworkers get paid less than local workers. They often get trapped in unskilled jobs, cut-off from the mainstream workforce. Many do not know their legal rights or feel brave enough to join trade unions. If they do not speak the language of their new country, they may not even understand that they are being paid less than local workers.

These Egyptian men are working in Kuwait. Kuwait has a shortage of workers and pays higher wages than the men could earn at home. As guestworkers, however, they have few political rights and can be ordered to leave the country at short notice.

Date:
2003
Place:
Wales, UK
Issue:
Fair wages

Paulo, an ex-shop steward, left his home in Portugal for the prospect of earning better pay in Wales. An agency had said he would earn £1200 a month for a 40-hour week, but Paulo found he earned only £3.60 an hour after deductions written into his contract were taken for transport and other charges. The agency also had him sign away any potential tax rebates to his company. However, Paulo has now found a permanent job in the UK, joined the Transport and General Workers' Union (TGWU) and is now recruiting his former colleagues to the union.

Paulo's case was one of several highlighted in a report titled 'Overworked, underpaid, and over here' published by the Trades Union Council in 2003. It said that 9% of the working population in the UK in 2002 was born outside the country, and this does not include those working illegally. Exploitative bosses pay migrant workers below the minimum wage and sometimes nothing. The TUC also noted that this precarious legal status means 'many end up working incredibly long hours for not much pay, in jobs that UK workers wouldn't want to do'. Those working illegally have no rights at all, since they cannot bring legal action.

'Those working illegally have no rights'

Even people in low paid jobs, such as pizza-delivery workers, have rights as long as they are not working illegally. Like many immigrant workers, Paulo was forced to work for a low wage and tricked into signing away benefits and his rights. Trades unions, such as the TGWU, can often help people find out what their rights are.

Fair pay – an ancient notion

The notion or idea of a fair wage is a very old one. In many agricultural communities around the world it was customary for the landlord or chief to host occasional feasts for his workers and to distribute new clothes and cash to them on special days of the year. This topped up the workers' earnings and ensured none was left destitute.

The Universal Declaration of Human Rights declares that everyone has the right to just and favourable remuneration (or

Queuing for unemployment benefit, like these people in New York, is an undignified and boring procedure, but social security payments are vital for many to avoid destitution.

reward) for their work, backed up where necessary by other means of social protection. This means that workers should be paid an amount which enables them to meet their living costs and that, where a wage does not do this, other means of financial support like social security or welfare should be given to them.

Minimum wages

Many governments approach the notion of a fair wage by setting a minimum wage, an amount which it has calculated is able to meet a worker's basic living costs. Often, as in Indonesia and the Philippines,

Harvest was a time of celebration, as in this 19th-century farming image. Landlords often handed out food and new clothes for workers – a way of topping up wages.

the minimum wages are breached and employers pay their workers much less than the law states. Even when they are not observed, however, minimum wages can stand as a goal that workers and trade unionists can aim for in their negotiations with employers.

Who misses out?

Unskilled workers and young people are more likely than most to miss out on getting fair pay. They are also less likely to belong to trade unions. As with equal pay (see page 29), immigrants, too, are vulnerable, particularly if they are illegal immigrants like Muhammad, because an employer can always threaten to have them deported if they complain. They have no bargaining power at all.

'getting fair pay'

Lacking skills

Unskilled workers are vulnerable to unfair rates of pay because they have nothing unique to recommend them to an employer. A trained person like an architect can demand a rate of pay that recognizes the years of education, expertise and experience that he or she is bringing to the job. An office cleaner, however, has little power to bargain with an employer because cleaning requires few skills and little experience.

Despite his hard work, this young boy in Honduras will be paid far less than an adult doing the same job.

With few choices open to them, young people and immigrants often take low-paid, unskilled jobs.

Still at home

Teenagers are often employed at unfair rates of pay because employers rely upon the fact that they are probably still living at home and do not have to support themselves. In Europe and North America the profitability of the fast-food industry, especially the big burger chains, depends upon the labour of teenagers who accept rates of pay that no independent adult could ever survive on.

TRADE UNIONS

Date:
8 May 1993
Place:
Nganjuk, Java, Indonesia
Issue:
The right for workers
to organize collectively

'striking in Indonesia was dangerous'

On 8 May 1993, a woman's battered body was discovered in the back streets of Nganjuk on the Indonesian island of Java. Her name was Marsinah and she used to work at PT Catur Putra Surya (a Swiss/Indonesian factory), making wristwatches for export to foreign countries. Why had she been killed?

Many factory workers in Indonesia earn only about 60 pence (US$1.00) a day which is not enough even for them to eat properly. The wages at Marsinah's factory were low, but if she complained by herself, her employers would simply sack her. So she persuaded all of the factory's workers to stop work together – to go on strike. She hoped that this might force the factory-owners to give the workers a pay-rise.

Marsinah was a brave woman. In the past, organizing a strike in Indonesia was dangerous. Strikes were forbidden by law, and striking workers were often beaten up and imprisoned. Even today the army can be called to force strikers back to work. No-one is certain who killed Marsinah, but everyone knows that she was murdered for her part in the strike. Her friends believe that she was killed by the army and that the Indonesian government secretly approved of her death.

Striking workers in Lima, Peru, are scattered by a high-powered water cannon. Against such brute force, it is hard for trade unions to organize and persist with strike action.

Asian shoe-factories like this one turn out millions of pairs of shoes for European and American feet every year. The selling price of the shoes will be many times higher than what the worker got paid for making them – but workers who protest about their wages may find themselves without a job.

A cheap source of labour

You may own something made by a worker like Marsinah. If you have a pair of trainers, they were probably made in Indonesia or a neighbouring country. Ninety-nine per cent of the world's sports shoes are made in China and South-East Asia. International companies manufacture in these countries because they want to produce their goods as cheaply as possible. Low-paid workers, who don't belong to trade unions and who won't go on strike, cut costs. However, a few international companies are beginning to work towards changing this. They refuse to use factories that do not allow their workers union rights.

Trade union rights

Industrialization in 19th-century Britain brought about the first trade unions. But factory workers and agricultural labourers who banded together to demand increases in wages were treated like criminals. It was only early in this century that governments in North America, Europe and Australasia accepted that trade unions had a useful role to play in protecting workers' well-being and the 1948 Declaration of Human Rights recognized this as a right. Workers in newly industrializing countries like Indonesia are now fighting the battle for union rights that workers in industrialized countries fought last century.

The struggle for trade union rights in industrialized countries began last century. This group of workers and reformers helped organize a matchmakers' strike in Britain in 1888.

Empowering the workers

The right for workers to form trade unions recognizes that, as individuals, workers have less power than employers. Employers control the hiring of workers and their wages and conditions of work. Working together in a trade union gives workers the strength of numbers. It helps control the power of employers so that irresponsible ones do not overwork or underpay their workers. However, trade unions need to use their power responsibly. It is no good demanding such high wages that a business is forced to close and the workers lose their jobs.

How does a trade union work?

Imagine a farmer in Kashmir who has an apple crop to pick. He knows several families who can pick apples speedily. One family charges 30 rupees a bag and a second family 20 rupees a bag. But a third family, who is desperate for work, offers to pick the apples for only 15 rupees. Word spreads, and soon other farmers will only pay 15 rupees a bag. The first and second families are forced to accept the new, lower rate.

Next year, however, the apple-picking families are smarter. They get together before the harvest starts and promise one another that they will all demand 30 rupees a bag to pick the apples. They have formed a union. As long as they stick together and no-one agrees secretly to accept less, they should be able to force the farmers to pay them the better rate.

Striking, like these US workers, is a trade union's most powerful weapon but it is generally only used as a last resort.

Issue:
Rural trade
unions
Place:
Grape-growing
plantations,
Sao Francisco
Valley, Brazil

The Sao Francisco Valley in Brazil is rich with fruit plantations and the landowners enjoy healthy profits. But workers in the valley's vineyards are poorly paid and many face health risks associated with spraying pesticides and fertilizers without wearing protective clothing or masks.

After long talks with the landowners, the Rural Workers' Union of Brazil negotiated a pay rise of 10 per cent for the grape-growers, paid overtime and improvements in safety conditions. The local union is proud of its success but aims to achieve more: 'We want better transport facilities; we want people working with pesticides to be paid extra.'

Trade union organizers have to ensure that they are following the wishes of their members. Voting, as in this union meeting in Calcutta, India, is one way of doing this.

What can trade unions do?

Apart from campaigning for better wages, trade unions can negotiate with employers to improve safety procedures, holiday benefits or canteen facilities. They can offer advice to individual workers who have been dismissed or badly treated. They can put pressure on governments for changes to the law, perhaps about maternity leave or minimum wages. If necessary, trade unions can fight to get the best redundancy pay-outs for workers who lose their jobs when a factory closes.

This Brazilian farmworker is endangering his health spraying crops without a protective mask. Trade unions seek to protect workers against this sort of danger.

Date:
2004
Place:
Japan
Issue:
Overwork

The Japanese word karoshi means 'death from overwork'. Most karoshi deaths occur as a result of work-related heart attacks. Since the first case of karoshi was reported in 1969, there has been an increase in the number of cases – some people believe as many as 10,000 in 2003 – although many still go unreported. One reason for these deaths could be the high number of Japanese working hours. On average men work 60 hours a week, compared to a maximum of 48 in Europe. Some companies have introduced limited measures to reduce the number of deaths. These include health examinations for employees whose overtime exceeds company guidelines.

Persistent overwork causes stress and other health problems.

Time off

The right to rest and leisure is about protecting workers from physical exhaustion. It is also about looking after workers' spiritual and

cultural life – allowing people time to be with their families and friends, to practise their religion and to pursue hobbies. It is an ancient right, represented by the tradition of keeping one day a week free for religious worship, such as Fridays for Muslims or Sundays for Christians.

Relaxing with family and friends is an important part of everybody's life. People who are overworked, tired and irritable do not make good or safe workers.

Many of the world's religions call upon their followers to give up one day a week to prayer, worship and contemplation, concentrating on God rather than making money.

'working, too hard'

The Industrial Revolution undermined workers' right to rest and leisure. Factories worked around the clock and workers' shifts became longer and longer. In 1847 it was considered a big improvement when the British government ruled that women and children could not work more than 10 hours a day. Unhappily, factory workers in newly industrializing countries today often suffer the long hours and absence of paid holidays that existed in the factories of 19th-century Europe.

Lack of exercise and stress-related illnesses threaten the health of many desk-bound executives.

With improved lighting in the 19th century, work could continue around the clock.

In big cities, it is often the casual workers who suffer. Working on a low hourly rate, they receive no pay if they are sick or want time off and often have to work 50 or 60 hours a week to earn enough to live on. At the other end of the employment scale, highly paid business executives frequently damage their health and family life through overwork. Heart attacks or strokes brought on by working too hard are common.

Different types of leave

The provision of different types of leave is related to other workers' rights. Maternity leave which enables women to return to their old job after having a baby helps to prevent sex discrimination in the workplace. Parental leave and other 'family-friendly' schemes contribute to an acceptable working environment. In Sweden and Germany, for example, all working parents can take paid time off from work to look after their children if they are ill.

Companies with good management-employee relations are increasingly adopting 'family-friendly' leave schemes.

Date:
2004
Place:
Carpet-weaving
factories, Uttar
Pradesh, India
Issue:
Child labour

Kamlesh's parents are poor. His father, crippled in a quarry accident, has not worked for years. His mother runs a roadside tea-stall. When Kamlesh turned 8, his parents handed him over to a contractor who was recruiting workers for a carpet manufacturer. The contractor gave Kamlesh's parents an advance of 500 rupees (about £10) on his wages for medicine for his father – an offer too good to refuse. Kamlesh had entered upon a

'underfed and sickly'

terrible life. With 14 other boys he worked for 12 hours a day in a dark, airless shed knotting carpets which were to be sold in Germany. He was underfed and sickly, and squatting in front of the loom all day began to stunt his legs. He was never paid.

After a year Kamlesh's parents began to worry that they had not heard from him. Kamlesh's father finally tracked him down in a factory 200 km away, but the carpet manufacturer refused to release him. He said that the interest on the advance and the cost of feeding Kamlesh had risen to 5000 rupees (£100), a sum his parents could never hope to raise.

About 300,000 boys work in the Indian carpet industry. Kamlesh was one of the lucky ones. Four years after his father's visit, labour inspectors raided the shed and released the children. Kamlesh was returned to his grateful family.

Squatting for 10 to 12 hours a day to make carpets, these young Indian boys will soon suffer stunted legs and damaged spines.

Childhood: a time for education and play

In 1948 (and again in 1989 in the Convention on the Rights of the Child) the United Nations declared that children have the right to social protection. This means that they should be able to grow up in a safe and healthy environment, with opportunities for education, play and enjoyment. Millions of children in the world are denied these rights by working from an early age. They are often forced to work or are working so hard that their education suffers and they have no time to play. A childhood without fun is not much of a childhood at all.

All children, like these in Zimbabwe, have the right to an education and to the time to play.

Why does child labour exist?

Employers hire children in preference to adults because they are cheap to employ and are too small to fight for themselves. In Niger 65 per cent of children aged between 5–14 are working, in Sierra Leone the figure is 57 per cent. In India alone there may be more than 60 million child labourers.

Child labour is banned in many countries but unscrupulous employers often evade the regulations. In India, for example, it is illegal for children under 15 to work unless it is for their own family's business. To get around this employers simply claim that their child workers are their nephews.

Preventing child labour

Governments around the world have a responsibility to protect children – Kamlesh was freed from his work by an inspector working for the Indian government – but many have limited resources to do this effectively. Child labour will continue in India and elsewhere until consumers stop buying products made by children. Child protection agencies in India have been working with responsible carpet manufacturers and European and American importers to set up a scheme of 'approved carpets' for sale overseas. These carpets would carry a label guaranteeing that they had been made without child labour.

Hammering for this small boy from Bangladesh is no game. He is already working for his living.

In the developed world, many teenagers work to top up their pocket money.

Saving money

Child labour is widespread in industrialized countries as well, although few children are forced to work against their will. In the USA, over 4 million teenagers have a summer job, and those aged 14 and 15 can work until 9pm. Companies who employ children save money by not having to employ adults on adult wages. Many businesses in Europe and North America would be less profitable if they did not employ teenagers.

In an attempt to ensure children are not exploited, in 1994 the European Parliament prohibited any child from working more than 12 hours a week and placed a total ban on children working at night. Laws like this form part of governments' role in upholding a child's 'right to social protection'.

The issue:
Ethical banking
The place:
Ohio, USA

Max Klemm had worked at a feed and grain store in Ohio since he was 18, but when he was 55 the store was closed down. Max received $74,000 for losing his job, which he decided to invest.

Max did not want his money to go to companies that damaged the environment or used child-labour or banned trade unions – something that is hard to avoid when so many big companies have factories all over the world. But Max went to an investment agency that specialized in ethical banking. Ethical banking means investing only in companies which do not make harmful products, damage the environment or treat their workers badly. Max wanted to be sure that his dollars wouldn't be hurting anyone anywhere in the world.

Investment from abroad has enabled countries like India to start to adopt new technology. Many now feel that overseas investors must ensure that their money is being used in an ethically correct way.

Generally, workers' rights are more secure and better observed in rich countries than in poor countries. This is not because the employers in poor countries are always worse than in rich countries. It has happened because of the history of economic development in the world.

The race for prosperity

The rich, industrialized countries of Europe, North America and Australasia had a head-start in the race for economic prosperity. They built up their industrial strengths in the 18th and 19th centuries when workers' rights were weak. Indeed, much of their prosperity was founded on exploiting the labour of slaves and early factory workers. The countries of Western Europe prospered by their ownership of colonies in Africa and Asia. They could afford to direct their workers away from farming and into factories only because their colonies were supplying them with food and raw products like wool and cotton.

Many of the workers' rights discussed in this book were established by workers in Europe and North America only after industrialization was well underway and only after numerous battles and confrontations with employers and governments. In many countries in Africa, Asia and Latin America these battles have only just begun.

Oil is one of the most valuable commodities in the world. For poor countries like Sudan the discovery of oil promises great riches, although the benefits do not always reach down to the workers.

Creating an even balance

People in rich countries cannot lecture poor countries about their bad treatment of workers without accepting some of the blame themselves. Cheap labour is often the only advantage that poor countries have over rich countries. It is unreasonable to expect them to implement improved conditions and pay for their workers if, by doing so, they lose the only advantage which enables them to sell goods to the industrialized world.

Workers' rights can only be improved in poor countries if the industrialized nations agree to assist them with money, education and technological advice to allow them to compete with the rich countries on a more equal footing. The wealthy owners of international companies will have to reduce the huge profits they make from their business concerns in poor countries. Consumers must be aware of the price in human terms other people are paying to produce an endless supply of cheap manufactured items.

A global outlook

The world we live in today is truly a global one. Our food, clothing, household items and entertainment come from all over the world. When the United Nations General Assembly met in 1948 to draw up the Universal Declaration of Human Rights, they had a vision of the world working as one. This vision is more relevant today than ever before. Workers' rights must be tackled on a global basis to achieve a just and humane workplace for workers, whatever country they may belong to.

'The world we live in today is truly a global one'

It makes financial sense to use cheap manual labour to build this dam in India rather than 'high-tech' machinery.

blue-collar job: a job requiring physical labour and endurance rather than mental skills; the jobs are often dirty, as on building sites or in factories, and are therefore called blue-collar jobs because of the blue protective overalls that manual workers often wear.

casual work: work done on an occasional basis, often part-time, with no fixed hours or rates of pay.

co-operative: a shop or business venture which is run and owned by the people who work in it; costs and profits are shared between the workers.

commerce: the world of finance and banking; the buying and selling of goods on a large scale.

Convention on the Rights of the Child: an international treaty made by the United Nations in 1989 stating the freedoms and provisions that all children should have, such as the freedom from abuse and the right to good healthcare and education. Only countries who agree to the convention have to follow it.

destitution: complete poverty; the condition of a person who does not have any form of shelter and has no way of earning money.

dignity: honour or pride in oneself; a person who is ashamed of their circumstances or feels that their life is useless has lost their dignity.

discrimination: the act of choosing one thing rather than another; in the world of employment, discrimination is used as a negative term to describe the rejecting of applicants for jobs because of who they are or what they look like.

equal opportunities: the chance for all applicants, regardless of their race or sex, to get the same job; a company with an equal opportunities policy is one which chooses its employees purely on the grounds of their skills; it does not discriminate against job applicants because they are female or from a minority community or physically disabled.

ethical: relating to ethics, the branch of philosophy concerned with ideas about right and wrong behaviour. If some thing or action is described as ethical, it is usually in accord with the approved moral standards of the time.

European Parliament: the parliament of the European Union; it is based in Strasbourg in France and makes laws which apply to the countries in the European Union; the Parliament's representatives are elected by the people in all the countries who belong to the European Union.

guestworker: a foreigner who works in another country, usually on a long-term but temporary basis, with the intention of returning to his or her home country in due course.

immigrant: a foreigner who has settled permanently in a new country.

information technology: the knowledge of machines and systems used to store and communicate information rapidly, such as computers, telephones and satellites.

legislation: laws; the act of making laws to determine what people can do in their country or community.

maternity leave: a break from work granted to a pregnant woman, so that she can have some time off both before the birth of her baby and afterwards, knowing that her old job will be kept for her to return to.

prosecute: to accuse someone before a legal court of breaking a specific law; to try to convince a court that someone has broken a law and should be punished.

public sector: the section of jobs in a country paid for by the state with money raised by taxes, for example, the police force or teachers in state education.

quota: a fixed share or proportion; quotas can be used to help establish employment patterns that match a country's population distribution. For example, if 5 per cent of a country's population was disabled, then its government might rule that companies should ensure that at least 5 per cent of the workers they hire were disabled. In some countries, including the UK, a similar system of targetting is used, where targets for employment ratios are set rather than quotas.

redundancy: the loss of a job through no fault of the worker; when workers are sacked because they are no longer needed by their company they have been made redundant. If a company bought a machine that required one person to operate it and did the same job that three people had previously done manually, the company would now only need one worker rather than three, so they might make two workers redundant.

remuneration: payment or reward for work done.

safety standards: rules set by an organization, such as a factory, local council or government, which establish the minimum requirements for providing a safe working environment for people; safety standards cover all sorts of hazards: fire, machinery, chemicals, ventilation and air quality, overwork and tiredness.

service industries: industries that do not produce actual physical products (like a car or a radio), but instead provide a service for people; banking, tourism and law are all service industries.

social security: the provision by a government of money and benefits to look after people who cannot earn enough to support themselves; state retirement pensions, national health schemes and state unemployment benefits are forms of social security.

telecommunications: the science that deals with long-distance communications, such as communication by satellite, electric telegraph, radio signals and fibre optics; 'tele' is a Greek word, meaning 'far off' or 'at a distance'.

trade union: an organization of workers who work in the same type of employment and who support each other in getting better wages and conditions from their employers.

United Nations (UN): the body of independent countries formed after the Second World War and designed to act like a world parliament; the founders of the UN hoped to use it to stop further wars and limit human suffering; all the independent nations of the world were expected to join and to try to attain standards of government set by the UN; the UN is funded by contributions from member countries.

welfare: happiness, comfort and security; because a government's social security provisions, such as unemployment benefit, are designed to achieve welfare for people, these provisions are sometimes called welfare for short, for example, 'The Jones family is on welfare.'

white-collar job: a job which, instead of physical skills, requires mental skills such as the ability to write letters, do accounts and keep records; white-collar jobs are usually office jobs; they are called white-collar jobs because they are fairly clean jobs and the men who used to do them traditionally wore white shirts instead of the protective clothing worn by workers in dirty, blue-collar jobs.

Useful addresses

Amnesty International, UK
99–119 Rosebery Avenue
London EC1R 4RE
www.amnesty.org.uk

Anti-Slavery International
Thomas Clarkson House
The Stableyard
Broomgrove Road
London SW9 9TL
www.antislavery.org

Trades Union Congress
Congress House
Great Russell Street
London WC1B 3LS
www.tuc.org.uk

Christian Aid
35 Lower Marsh
London SE1 7RL
www.christian-aid.org.uk

Oxfam
Oxfam House
274 Banbury Road
Oxford OX2 7DZ
www.oxfam.org.uk

Australian Industrial Relations
Commission
Level 35, Nauru House
80 Collins Street
Melbourne VIC 3000
Australia
www.airc.gov.au

Amnesty International, Australia
29 Shepherd Street
Chippendale NSW 2008
Australia
www.amnesty.org.au

Australian Red Cross
155 Pelham Street
Carlton VIC 3053
Australia
www.redcross.org.au

Workcover New South Wales
Locked Bag 2906
Lisarow NSW 2252
Australia
www.workcover.nsw.gov.au

INDEX